Transforming Managers into Catalysts for Team Success

MA. LUIS JASA-LOQUE "Imaan"

DEDICATION

To all the managers and leaders who work to create high-performing teams and promote organizational success, I dedicate this book on turning managers into catalysts for team success. Building a collaborative environment and enabling team members to realize their full potential depend on your commitment, leadership, and drive for continual development.

TRANSFORMING MANAGERS INTO CATALYSTS FOR TEAM SUCCESS

This book is dedicated to managers who set a good example, encourage a team mentality, give their team members responsibility, and support a continuous improvement culture. Your work has a big impact on the accomplishments of your team and helps your company expand and succeed.

Thank you for turning managers become catalysts for team success via your commitment, leadership, and dedication. I wrote this book with you in mind.

To my beloved daughters, Angie, Angela and Amanda, I dedicate all my hard work and efforts to provide you with a better future. Your love and support have been my inspiration and motivation to strive for excellence in everything I do. I hope this book on transforming managers into catalysts for team success serve as an example of the value of hard work, dedication, and leadership and inspires you to pursue your dreams with passion and determination. Thank you for being my angels and for making my life brighter everyday.

TRANSFORMING MANAGERS INTO CATALYSTS FOR TEAM SUCCESS

CONTENTS

Table of Contents

ACKNOWLEDGMENTS

I would like to express my sincere gratitude to all those who have contributed to the creation and success of this book on transforming managers into catalysts for team success.

First and foremost to Allah (SWT) for giving me the knowledge and wisdom to write this book, " Transforming Managers into Catalysts for Team Success:.

TRANSFORMING MANAGERS INTO CATALYSTS FOR TEAM SUCCESS

To all of my previous supervisors and managers, with whom I have worked since I began at the age of 20, particularly the following:

Mr. Orlando Verniz, who taught me how to be a leader instead of being a manager. His leadership approach inspires his team to work for a future vision that is both clear and compelling.

Dean Carol Lozano, who saw potential in me as a leader even when I was a freshly appointed faculty member many years ago.

Mr. Richard Regala seeks input from his team members and incorporates them into decision-making processes. He also takes into account our abilities, skills, and talent.

Rehana Al Ameer, my first employer while working abroad who instilled in me the importance of becoming a leader with compassion

Zayana Al Sinawi is a leader who prioritizes silently carrying out her duties rather than whining. Her leadership has taught me to put the needs of the team members and to seek to foster an environment where the team can succeed.

Noora Al Hoqani, a leader who stood up for the right of her team member. She showed compassion and allowed her team members to express their ideas freely.

Najma Al Bimani, whose leadership cultivates a compelling vision and a feeling of purpose in her team members to drive them toward higher levels of performance and achievement. She challenges her team members to think creatively, accept change, and challenge the status quo

Working with you all taught me many different leadership philosophies, which made this book complete. Thank you for sharing your wisdom and experiences.

.

1 INTRODUCTION

Any organization's management team must function effectively for it to be successful. It is the responsibility of managers to guide their teams in achieving the aims and objectives of the organization. Control and command-based management styles have dominated traditional management methods, which can impede team success. Organizations now need a different sort of manager—one who can serve as a catalyst for the success of their team—in the fast-paced business climate.

TRANSFORMING MANAGERS INTO CATALYSTS FOR TEAM SUCCESS

A material that accelerates a chemical reaction without being eaten is known as a catalyst. A manager who gives their team the support, direction, and resources they need to reach their greatest potential is known in the management world as a catalyst. Catalyst managers cultivate a culture that encourages collaboration, originality, and innovation, which improves organizational results.

A change in management strategy is necessary to transform managers into engines for team success. Managers need to have a team mentality, empower their staff, foster collaboration, set a positive example, foster a culture of continuous improvement, and be open to making changes. The managers themselves profit from this transformation in addition to the organization as a whole. Increased job satisfaction, greater levels of engagement, and better performance can all result from a team-centric strategy.

.

2 UNDERSTANDING THE ROLES OF A CATALYST

Understanding the role of a catalyst is the first step in transforming managers into team success catalysts. In this chapter, we will look at the concept of a catalyst and how it can be used in management. We'll talk about the characteristics of a catalyst, such as adaptability, creativity, and empathy. We will also look at the advantages of being a team success catalyst, such as increased productivity, morale, and job satisfaction.

What is a Catalyst?

A catalyst is a substance that accelerates a chemical reaction without being consumed in the process. A catalyst in management is a manager who facilitates and accelerates team goals and objectives without dominating or micromanaging team members. A catalyst manager serves as a facilitator, coach, and supporter for their team, fostering creativity, innovation, and collaboration. Catalyst leaders empower their teams, foster trust and respect, and foster a culture of continuous learning and improvement.

Characteristics of a Catalyst

Managers must have certain characteristics that allow them to facilitate and accelerate team performance in order to be a catalyst for team success. Among these characteristics are:

1. Adaptability: A catalyst manager must be able to adjust their management style to meet the needs of their team in the face of changing circumstances.

2. Creativity: A catalyst manager must be creative in order to inspire their team members to think creatively. This can lead to more creative problem-solving and better outcomes.

3. Empathy: A catalyst manager must be able to empathize

with and understand their team members' needs, concerns, and perspectives. This can help to foster a supportive and inclusive environment by fostering trust and respect within the team.

4. A catalyst manager must maintain a positive attitude and set a good example. A positive attitude can help to motivate team members and foster an optimistic and resilient culture.

Benefits of Being a Catalyst for Team Success

Being a catalyst for team success has a number of advantages for both the team and the organization. Among these advantages are:

1. Increased Productivity: A catalyst manager can assist in increasing team productivity by providing the necessary support, guidance, and resources for team members to reach their full potential.

2. Improved Morale: By creating a supportive and inclusive environment that values diversity and promotes equity, a catalyst manager can help to improve team morale.

3. Greater Job Satisfaction: By empowering team members and providing opportunities for growth and development, a

catalyst manager can help to increase team members' job satisfaction.

4. Better Team Performance: By encouraging creativity, innovation, and collaboration, a catalyst manager can help to improve team performance.

A real-life example of a catalyst's role in the workplace could be as follows:

Samantha oversees a team of software developers. Samantha noticed that team members were feeling demotivated and disengaged as they struggled to meet project deadlines recently. She recognized that the team required a catalyst to help them overcome these obstacles and get back on track.

Samantha decided to take on the role of team catalyst. She started by encouraging open and honest communication among team members, allowing them to freely express their concerns and ideas. She also encouraged creative thinking by having the team brainstorm new approaches to the project.

Samantha demonstrated her adaptability by recognizing that

some team members were having difficulty with specific tasks and providing additional training and resources to help them improve. She also demonstrated empathy for team members by recognizing and responding to their personal and professional needs. She, for example, gave a team member who was struggling with child care responsibilities flexible work hours.

Samantha's efforts helped the team feel more engaged, motivated, and supported. They collaborated to develop innovative solutions to project challenges, which resulted in better results. Samantha continued to help the team by giving regular feedback and recognizing individual and team accomplishments.

Samantha's efforts resulted in the team completing the project ahead of schedule, and team members reported feeling more satisfied and fulfilled in their roles. Samantha's role as a catalyst was critical to the team's success and contributed to the creation of a positive and productive work environment.

The first step toward becoming a catalyst for team success is to understand the role of a catalyst. Catalyst managers enable and accelerate team performance by empowering team members, fostering trust and respect, and fostering a culture of continuous learning and improvement. They have characteristics such as adaptability, creativity, empathy, and a positive attitude that allow them to foster an environment that promotes teamwork, creativity, and innovation. Being a catalyst for team success can result in increased productivity, morale, job satisfaction, and improved performance, which benefits both the team and the organization.

3 DEVELOPING A TEAM MINDSET

Developing a team mindset is critical for managers who want to transform themselves into team success catalysts. A team mindset is a shared point of view that values collaboration, cooperation, and group success. It entails accepting that the whole team is greater than the sum of its parts and that everyone has a role to play in achieving team objectives. In this chapter, we will look at the advantages of cultivating a team mindset as well as strategies for managers to foster a team-oriented culture.

Benefits of Developing a Team Mindset

Developing a team mindset can have numerous advantages for the team as well as the organization. Here are some of the advantages of cultivating a team mindset:

1. Improved Collaboration: A team mindset encourages team members to collaborate and cooperate. When members of a team work together toward a common goal, they can achieve more significant results than if they worked alone.

2. Enhanced Creativity: A team mindset encourages creativity and innovation by allowing team members to share their ideas and perspectives. Different points of view can lead to more creative problem-solving solutions.

3. Accountability: A team mindset encourages accountability among team members. Team members are more likely to take ownership of their work and deliver high-quality results when they feel responsible for the team's success.

4. Increased Resilience: A team mindset fosters resilience by fostering a supportive and inclusive environment. Team members are more likely to recover from setbacks and challenges when they feel supported and valued.

Strategies for Developing a Team Mindset

1. Set Clear Goals: Managers should set clear, measurable goals for their teams and effectively communicate them to team members. Clear goals give the team a common purpose and a shared understanding of what success looks like.

2. Encourage Open Communication: Managers should encourage team members to communicate openly and honestly. They should provide a safe environment for team members to express their thoughts and ideas, seek assistance, and provide feedback.

3. Managers should encourage collaboration by assigning tasks that require team members to collaborate toward a common goal. They should also recognize and reward collaboration and teamwork.

4. Managers should build trust by being transparent, dependable, and consistent in their actions and decisions.

They should also have faith in their team members to take ownership of their work and make independent decisions.

5. Managers should provide the necessary support and resources to enable team members to achieve their objectives. They should also provide guidance and feedback to team members in order to help them improve their performance.

6. Managers should celebrate team and individual successes to reinforce the team's common goal and to foster a culture of recognition and appreciation.

Developing a team mindset is essential for team success. A team mindset fosters collaboration, creativity, accountability, and resilience, which benefits the team as well as the organization. Managers can foster a team mindset by establishing clear goals, encouraging open communication, encouraging collaboration, developing trust, offering support, and celebrating success.

Managers can create a culture that values teamwork, promotes innovation, and achieves exceptional results by becoming catalysts for developing a team mindset.

The study conducted by Lu, Wang, and Wu (2020) on the effects of team mindset on team innovation in the context of research and development teams is one example of developing a team mindset. The study discovered that a team mindset, defined by a shared belief in the value of collaboration, led to higher levels of team innovation.

The researchers surveyed 294 members of Chinese research and development teams for the study. They assessed team mindset by asking participants to rate their level of agreement with statements like "Collaboration is essential to our team's success" and "We work as a team to achieve our goals." They assessed team innovation by asking participants to rate their team's ability to generate new ideas, implement new processes, and create new products.

Teams with a strong team mindset had significantly higher levels of team innovation than teams with a weak team mindset, according to the findings. According to the researchers, a team mindset fosters a culture of collaboration and trust, allowing team members to feel comfortable sharing their ideas and taking risks. This leads to increased levels of team innovation.

This study provides empirical evidence of the advantages of cultivating a team mindset for team success. Managers can use the findings of this study to help them promote a team-oriented culture that values collaboration, trust, and innovation

4 EMPOWERING TEAM

Empowering your team entails giving them the tools, resources, and support they need to take ownership of their work and make independent decisions. Teams that are empowered are more engaged, productive, and innovative, which leads to better results for the organization. In this section, we will look at the benefits of empowering your team and provide managers with strategies for doing so effectively.

Benefits of Empowering Your Team

The benefits of empowering your team can be numerous for both the team and the organization. Some of the advantages of empowering your team are as follows:

1. Improved Productivity: Because empowered teams have the autonomy to make decisions and take ownership of their work, they are more productive.

2. Enhanced Engagement: Empowered teams are more engaged because they believe their managers value and trust them. This can result in higher job satisfaction and lower turnover rates.

3. Increased Innovation: Because they have the freedom to experiment and take risks, empowered teams are more innovative. This can result in novel ideas and approaches that benefit the organization.

4. Greater Accountability: Because they are accountable for their work and decisions, empowered teams are more accountable. This can lead to improved performance and outcomes for the organization.

Strategies for Empowering Your Team

Managers can use the following strategies to empower their teams:

1. Managers should delegate authority to team members so that they can make decisions and take ownership of their work. Giving them the freedom to choose how they work, who they work with, and how they solve problems is one example.

2. Provide Resources: Managers should provide team members with the resources and tools they need to do their jobs effectively. Training, coaching, and access to technology and equipment are all examples of this.

3. Encourage Creativity: Managers should encourage creativity by giving team members opportunities to

share their ideas and perspectives. They should also recognize and reward originality and creativity.

4. Managers can build trust by being transparent, honest, and consistent in their actions and decisions. They should also have faith in their team members' ability to make decisions and take responsibility for their work.

Managers should provide guidance, feedback, and recognition to team members in order to help them improve their performance. They should also be available to answer questions and help when necessary.

Managers should celebrate team and individual successes in order to strengthen the team's sense of accomplishment and to promote a culture of recognition and appreciation.

The case study conducted by Morrison and Milliken (2000) on the transformation of a traditional manufacturing company, Sundown, into a successful and innovative organization by empowering its employees is one real-life scenario of team empowerment. According to the study, empowering employees through training, trust, and recognition resulted in higher levels of employee engagement, creativity, and job satisfaction, which led to improved organizational performance.

Sundown was experiencing declining sales and profitability as a result of increased competition and a lack of innovation, according to the study. The management decided to empower its employees by providing training and development opportunities, increasing their autonomy, recognizing and rewarding their contributions, and fostering a culture of trust and collaboration.

According to the findings, empowered employees were more engaged and committed to the organization. They were also more creative and innovative, which resulted in the development of new products and processes that increased sales and profitability. According to the findings of the study, empowering employees is a critical factor in organizational success, especially in dynamic and competitive environments.

This case study demonstrates the advantages of

empowering employees in the transformation of traditional organizations into innovative and successful ones. Managers can use the findings of this study to help them promote employee empowerment through training, trust, recognition, and collaboration.

Empowering your team is essential for team success. Teams that are empowered are more engaged, productive, and innovative, which leads to better results for the organization. Managers can empower their teams by delegating authority, providing resources, fostering trust, providing support, and celebrating success. Managers who act as catalysts for team empowerment can foster a culture that values autonomy, creativity, and accountability, resulting in exceptional results..

5 BUILDING A CULTURE OF COLLABORATION

The manager is responsible for fostering a collaborative culture because it is crucial for team success. In this chapter, we'll talk about creating a collaborative environment that encourages team members to share ideas and work together to achieve common objectives.

The success of a team depends critically on the culture of collaboration that is created. With collaboration, team members can work together toward a similar objective while utilizing one another's skills and knowledge to produce superior outcomes. In this section, we'll examine the advantages of teamwork and offer managers tips for building a

cooperative environment in their workplaces.

Benefits of Collaboration

Both individuals and organizations can profit much from

collaboration. Here are a few advantages of cooperation:

1. Increased Communication: Collaboration fosters open

   and honest discussion among team members, which

   improves communication. Better decision-making and

   problem-solving may result from this.

2. Collaboration encourages creativity by allowing team

   members to express their thoughts and opinions, which

   leads to creative solutions.

3. Collaboration can boost productivity by enabling team

   members to draw on one another's skills and

   knowledge, which results in quicker and more effective

   work.

4. Increased Engagement: By giving team members a sense of ownership and participation to the organization's goals, collaboration can improve engagement.

5. Better Quality Results: By ensuring that everyone on the team is focusing on the same objective, collaboration can produce results that are of a higher caliber.

Strategies for Building a Culture of Collaboration

Managers can use the following tactics to create a collaborative culture:

1. Establish Specific Objectives: Team leaders should provide their workers with specific objectives and guidelines. The team's goal, vision, and objectives, as

well as the duties and responsibilities of each team member, can be defined as part of this process.

2. Build Trust: By being open, truthful, and consistent in their behaviors and decisions, managers should foster trust. Also, team members should be encouraged to communicate honestly and openly.

3. Promote Diversity: Managers should promote an inclusive culture that supports many viewpoints and ideas in order to encourage variety. This can involve giving team members the chance to express their thoughts and viewpoints and offering training on diversity and cultural awareness.

4. Give Resources: Managers should give team members the resources and equipment they need to collaborate successfully. These may include tools, instruction, and

assistance.

5. Acknowledge and Praise Collaboration: Managers should recognize and praise collaboration by praising both the efforts of the team as a whole and the individual team members. These can include pay raises, public acclaim, and bonuses for performance.

6. Encourage Team Building: Supervisors should support team building exercises that foster cooperation and communication. These can involve social gatherings, team-building activities, and instruction on efficient communication and collaboration

For a team to succeed, a collaborative culture must be created. With collaboration, team members can work together toward a similar objective while utilizing one another's skills and knowledge to produce superior outcomes. By establishing clear objectives, developing trust, supporting diversity, giving resources, recognizing and rewarding collaboration, and encouraging team-building exercises, managers can create a

collaborative culture. Managers may foster a team environment

that values communication, diversity, and teamwork and

produce extraordinary results by taking the lead in fostering the

development of a collaborative culture..

6 LEADING BY EXAMPLE

A leader who sets an example by acting in a way they want their followers to follow is said to be leading by example. This leadership approach works well because it fosters a climate of trust, respect, and accountability, which boosts output and produces better results. We will discuss the advantages of leading by example in this section and present examples, citations, and references to support this leadership philosophy.

Benefits of Leading by Example

There are numerous benefits of leading by example including:

1. Building Trust: When leaders lead by example, they show their dedication to the objectives and values of the company. This fosters a culture of respect and trust among followers, which boosts cooperation and production.

2. Others' Inspiration: When leaders set an exemplary example, they encourage others to do the same. As a result, followers may be more motivated and engaged, which will improve their performance and results.

3. A culture of responsibility is created when leaders provide an exemplary example for others to follow. Because of this, there is greater decision-making and problem-solving across the board because everyone in

the organization is accountable for their actions and
behaviors.

4. Building Respect: When leaders set an exemplary
   example for their followers, they gain their respect. As
   a result, the workplace becomes more cheerful and
   polite, which boosts employee retention and job
   satisfaction..

Here are some instances of leaders who have done a good
job of setting an example:

1. Gandhi was a leader who set an example for others to
   follow. He led a straightforward, modest life as proof
   of his dedication to nonviolence and civil disobedience.
   Millions of people were motivated by this to fight for
   Indian freedom by following in his footsteps.

2. Steve Jobs: Jobs was an inspirational leader. He had a
   strong work ethic and an eye for detail, which revealed

his enthusiasm for design and creativity. His team was motivated by this to produce some of the tech sector's most ground-breaking goods.

3. Ellen DeGeneres: DeGeneres is a role model for others to follow. She is renowned for being compassionate and kind, and she exhibits these qualities via her philanthropic endeavors and humanitarian activities. This has motivated countless individuals to emulate her and have a great influence on their communities.

4. Sayyid Asaad bin Tariq Al Said, the Special Representative of His Majesty Sultan Haitham bin Tariq Al Said and the Deputy Prime Minister for Foreign Relations and Cooperative Affairs, is an example of a leader in Oman who leads by example. Sayyid Asaad has proven his dedication to the

advancement of Oman via his leadership, work ethic,
and commitment.

Sayyid Asaad is renowned for his hands-on leadership
style and has been involved in numerous projects and
initiatives that have aided in the expansion and
development of Oman. He was instrumental in the
creation of the Duqm Special Economic Zone, a
significant infrastructural undertaking that has attracted
billions of dollars in investment and produced
thousands of employment.

An effective leadership style is one that sets an example for
followers and encourages their respect, trust, and
responsibility. Leaders who provide an example for others to
follow by living out the organization's beliefs and goals
encourage them to do the same. Mahatma Gandhi, Steve Jobs,
and Ellen DeGeneres are a few examples of leaders who have
done a good job of setting an example. Citations and
references back up the advantages of setting a good example

for others, which include developing a culture of respect and trust, motivating better levels of performance, and encouraging responsibility and accountability. When leaders set a good example for their followers, they foster a productive work atmosphere that produces better results.

There is a wealth of research that supports the benefits of leading by example. Here are some examples:

1. A study by Simons and Peterson (2000) found that leaders who lead by example are more effective in creating a culture of trust and respect among their followers.

2. A study by Gino and Pierce (2010) found that leaders who lead by example are more effective in inspiring their followers to achieve higher levels of performance.

3. A study by Hoyt and Blascovich (2016) found that leaders who lead by example are more effective in creating a culture of accountability and responsibility.

TRANSFORMING MANAGERS INTO CATALYSTS FOR TEAM SUCCESS

7 CREATING A CULTURE OF CONTINOUS IMPROVEMENT

For teams to succeed, cultivating a culture of continual improvement is crucial. We will talk about how to establish a culture of continuous improvement in this chapter, including how to promote learning and growth, pinpoint problem areas, acknowledge accomplishments, and take lessons from mistakes. We will also look at ways to foster an atmosphere that encourages creativity and experimentation.

Emphasize the Importance of Feedback and Communication

Stressing the value of communication and feedback is one of the cornerstones to developing a culture of continuous improvement. It can be helpful to find opportunities for development and innovation to encourage staff to offer their thoughts and suggestions for improvement. Google is an illustration of a business that prioritizes feedback and communication. Google has a culture that encourages staff members to share ideas and work together on projects. In order to better its products and services, Google also employs a range of tools and techniques, including surveys and town hall meetings.

Develop a Growth Mindset

Having a growth mentality is another essential element for fostering a culture of continual progress. This entails accepting obstacles, growing from setbacks, and looking for chances to advance. Amazon is one business that exemplifies a growth attitude by encouraging staff members to try new things and take calculated risks. To support their continued learning and development, Amazon offers its workers a variety of training and development options..

Foster a Culture of Collaboration

Another crucial component of developing a culture of continuous improvement is collaboration. Employee collaboration and knowledge sharing can lead to the creation of fresh concepts and ways to problem-solving. IBM is one firm that promotes a collaborative environment and encourages its staff to form cross-functional teams to tackle challenging issues. IBM supports its employees' collaborative efforts by utilizing a variety of collaboration tools and techniques, including online collaboration platforms and virtual brainstorming sessions.

Encourage Experimentation and Innovation

Developing a culture of continuous improvement also requires encouraging creativity and experimentation. Allowing workers the freedom to take chances and try new things can result in innovations and discoveries. Apple, known for being a

very innovative firm, is one example of a business that
promotes experimentation and innovation. Apple encourages
its staff to think creatively and unconventionally when solving
issues. Several ground-breaking products, including the iPhone
and iPad, have resulted from this strategy..

Provide Opportunities for Learning and Development.

Finally, fostering a culture of continuous improvement requires
offering opportunities for growth and learning. This entails
funding employee development and training programs and
fostering a conducive learning environment. Microsoft, which
provides its employees with a variety of training and
development options, is one example of a business that
prioritizes learning and development. Additionally, Microsoft
has a culture that supports continual learning and
development, and it gives its employees access to a variety of
tools and resources to help them continue to grow and
develop..

TRANSFORMING MANAGERS INTO CATALYSTS FOR TEAM
SUCCESS

Organizations that wish to be competitive and inventive must cultivate a culture of continual development. Organizations can develop a culture that supports continuous growth and development by highlighting the value of feedback and communication, fostering a growth mindset, fostering a culture of collaboration, encouraging experimentation and innovation, and offering opportunities for learning and development. The examples and sources mentioned earlier.

Here are some more examples of organizations that have successfully created a culture of continuous improvement:

1. Toyota: The "kaizen" principle of continual improvement, which is engrained in the company's culture, is well-known for Toyota. With this strategy, processes and products are gradually improved in modest, incremental steps in an effort to increase quality and efficiency. Toyota has built a number of procedures and systems to assist continuous improvement, including the "andon" system, which

38

gives workers the authority to halt the manufacturing line if they see a quality problem. Toyota encourages all employees to participate in this process.

2. Procter & Gamble: P&G's corporate culture is ingrained with a long-standing dedication to continual improvement. The business has a program called "Connect+Develop" that encourages staff members to communicate and work together across divisions and locations. In order to promote continuous improvement in its operations and products, P&G also employs a range of techniques and methodologies, including Six Sigma and Lean.

3. QuickBooks and TurboTax creator Intuit has an innovative and experimental culture that encourages staff members to take calculated chances and learn from failure. The business has put in place a number of procedures to foster this culture, like recurring "innovation weeks" where staff members can work on fresh concepts aside from their regular duties.

Additionally, Intuit employs data analytics and user input to guide its attempts at continual improvement.

4. General Electric: Since the time of venerable CEO Jack Welch, GE has a long history of constant development. Lean and Six Sigma are only a couple of the approaches and frameworks the company has adopted to promote continuous improvement throughout all of its businesses. GE also employs digital tools and data analytics to pinpoint problem areas and monitor development over time.

5. Zappos: The online shoe and apparel shop Zappos has a culture that prioritizes innovation and constant development. In order to promote this culture, the company has devised a number of procedures, such as "Zapponian" training, which trains staff members to uphold the company's values and goals. In order to discover fresh approaches to enhance the client experience, Zappos also pushes staff to take chances and try novel things.

Here are some examples of organizations in Oman that have created a culture of continuous improvement:

1. Oman Air: Oman Air, the national airline of Oman, has a strong culture of ongoing improvement, which has aided it in achieving high levels of client satisfaction and operational effectiveness. The business has established a number of initiatives to support this culture, including the "Customer First" program, which encourages staff to concentrate on satisfying customer needs, and the "Savings and Ideas" program, which enables staff to submit ideas for streamlining procedures and cutting costs.

2. A significant oil and gas business in Oman, Petroleum Development Oman (PDO), has a long-standing dedication to continuous improvement that is ingrained in its corporate culture. In order to support this culture, the company has established a number of initiatives and programs, including the "Lean Six Sigma" program, which uses data and analysis to identify areas for

improvement, and the "PDO Way" program, which motivates staff to take charge of the continuous improvement process.

3. The biggest bank in Oman, Bank Muscat, has a culture of constant improvement that is motivated by a dedication to creativity and client satisfaction. In order to foster this culture, the company has launched a variety of programs, including the "Customer Delight" program and the "Quality Circle" program, both of which encourage staff to collaborate in identifying areas for development.

4. The largest telecommunications company in Oman, Omantel, has put in place a continuous improvement program called "Taqdeer" that emphasizes giving employees the tools they need to recognize and address issues. The program offers training on problem-solving techniques and encourages staff members to contribute suggestions for improvement. The program, according to Omantel, has significantly increased productivity and

customer satisfaction.

5. Oman Refineries and Petrochemicals Company
   (ORPIC): ORPIC, the country of Oman's national oil
   refining and petrochemicals firm, has put in place a
   continuous improvement program dubbed "i-Enhance"
   with the goal of enhancing efficiency, dependability,
   and safety. The course covers problem-solving and
   Lean technique training, as well as tools for finding
   improvement possibilities like process mapping and
   data analysis. The program, according to ORPIC, has
   resulted in considerable increases in safety,
   dependability, and cost savings.

8 IMPLEMENTING CHANGE

Change implementation can be difficult, especially in workplaces where employees are opposed to it. Yet, successful change management may guide organizations through the process of putting change into action. The steps involved in implementing change will be covered in this section, along with examples of businesses that have done so successfully.

Creating an urgency for change is the first step in the implementation process. This entails explaining to the staff why the change is essential and what the potential repercussions of doing nothing about it might be. For instance, if a company is developing a new customer relationship management system, it may inform staff that the existing system is antiquated and unreliable and that switching to the new system will boost client happiness and income.

Putting together a coalition of support is the next step. This entails locating important players who can promote the change and increase support for it. For instance, if a company is putting in place a new performance management system, they can look for managers who are already on board with the change and ask them to assist in explaining its advantages to their employees.

The third phase is to develop a change's vision. This entails developing a compelling vision for the future of the organization once the change has been accomplished. For instance, if a company is launching a new sustainability project, they may come up with a vision statement that expresses their resolve to lessen their carbon footprint and develop into a more environmentally conscious company.

The sharing of the vision is the fourth phase. To accomplish this, the vision must be clearly, consistently, and effectively communicated to the workforce. Many communication methods, including town hall meetings, email updates, and video, might be used to accomplish this.

Action empowerment is the fifth step. This entails removing roadblocks that can stop employees from putting the change into action and giving them the tools and support they need to succeed. An organization might train staff members on how to use the new system and designate a project manager, for instance, if it is putting in place a new project management system..

Walmart is one instance of a company that effectively implemented change. Walmart introduced a sustainability initiative in 2005 with the goal of lowering waste, saving resources, and improving energy effectiveness. The

corporation pledged to eventually use only renewable energy
and to cut its greenhouse gas emissions by 20% by the year
2012.

The sustainability program at Walmart included a number
of measures, such as the use of renewable energy, a decrease in
packaging waste, and the introduction of more environmentally
friendly products. The business encouraged its suppliers to
adopt more environmentally friendly practices and lessen their
own environmental impacts by including them in the change
process.

Walmart created a "Sustainability Index" that detailed the
environmental impact of the goods sold in its stores in order to
convey the significance of sustainability to its staff. In order to
educate staff on the value of sustainability and to motivate
them to identify ways to cut waste and conserve resources at
work, the company also developed a training program.

Walmart was able to significantly lower its energy use and

greenhouse gas emissions as a result of these efforts. The corporation also made millions of dollars in savings through reducing waste and boosting productivity.

One example of an organization in Oman that successfully executed change is the Oman Oil Refineries and Petroleum Industries Company (ORPIC). Leading oil and gas firm in Oman, ORPIC has recently implemented a number of measures to enhance business processes and lessen environmental effect.

The adoption of a comprehensive energy management system (EnMS), which includes a number of energy-saving measures and the creation of an energy-conservation culture throughout the company, was one of ORPIC's important efforts. The EnMS comprised actions including maximizing energy utilization in the business's premises, setting up energy-efficient machinery, and utilizing renewable energy sources.

TRANSFORMING MANAGERS INTO CATALYSTS FOR TEAM SUCCESS

An elaborate training and awareness program for its staff was started by ORPIC to support the EnMS deployment. The program's objectives were to encourage energy conservation and foster a culture of continuous improvement. In order to raise awareness of the value of energy saving and to persuade them to adopt more environmentally friendly practices, the company also engaged with its stakeholders, including its customers, suppliers, and neighborhood communities.

With the help of these initiatives, ORPIC was able to significantly increase its energy efficiency and lessen its environmental effect. The business received numerous awards for its environmental performance and dedication to sustainable development as a result of its sustainability efforts.

9 CONCLUSION

In summary, creating high-performing teams that can propel organizational success requires managers to evolve into catalysts for team success. A catalyst manager sets a good example, fosters teamwork, gives team members autonomy, and encourages continuous growth. Managers can learn how to be successful catalysts and improve team performance through exercises and case studies.

TRANSFORMING MANAGERS INTO CATALYSTS FOR TEAM SUCCESS

Managers may enable their teams to perform to their maximum potential by understanding the function of a catalyst, fostering a culture of collaboration, empowering team members, and cultivating a team mindset. Teams can succeed more and contribute to the organization's growth and success overall with the appropriate leadership style.

Overall, switching from a traditional top-down management style to one that is more collaborative and empowering is necessary to be a catalyst manager. Managers may create a culture of success and create teams that are highly motivated, creative, and productive by investing in the development of their management abilities and adopting a catalyst attitude.

10 CASE STUDIES

Case Study 1: Building a Collaborative Team

Scenario: You have been tasked with creating a team that is imaginative, collaborative, and high-performing as a recently appointed manager. Individuals with various backgrounds and skill sets make up your team.

Activity: To do this, you choose to hold a team-building activity that encourages cooperation and cooperation. You organize a team-building exercise where participants cooperate to find a solution.

Result: A challenge that the group can tackle collectively

should be the focus of the team-building exercise. For instance, the group could work on a project where they would need to assign duties, generate ideas, and collaborate to reach a common objective. The team's communication will be boosted and trust will be increased as a result of this exercise. Also, it will inspire people to work together and play to their strengths in order to accomplish shared objectives.

Case Study 2: Empowering Team Members

Scenario: You oversee a group of people with a variety of backgrounds and specialties. You think that team members ought to have more freedom and authority to decide things that will affect their work. You worry, though, that they might not be prepared for this amount of responsibility..

Activity: You make the decision to assign more responsibilities to your team members and give them more authority over their work in an effort to empower them. Moreover, you exhort them to take charge of their endeavors and create choices that will have an influence on their career.

Result: Managers should give team members more authority over their work, assign them more responsibilities, and promote project ownership in order to empower them. This will motivate team members to take initiative and make them feel more accountable for their work. In order to help team members get the knowledge and self-assurance they need to take on more responsibility, managers can also offer criticism and support.

Case Study 3: Continuous Improvement

Scenario: You are in charge of a group that is in charge of providing clients with a product. You think that both the final result and the team's procedures can be improved. The crew, however, is averse to change, so you must find a way to inspire them to accept constant development.

Activity: You choose to establish a feedback loop where team members can offer comments on the product and the team's processes in order to encourage your team to embrace continuous improvement. Also, you foster a culture where team members are urged to try out novel concepts and take calculated risks.

Result: Managers should establish a feedback loop where team members can offer comments on the final product and the team's working procedures in order to encourage continual improvement. Managers may foster an environment where team members feel free to try out novel concepts and take reasonable risks. This will support the group in embracing change and enhancing its operational procedures consistently. Also, supervisors can offer assistance and resources to team members who are putting new concepts and projects into practice.

Here are some activities that managers can execute to transform themselves into catalysts for team success:

1. Assess your leadership style: Make a sincere evaluation of your leadership style and note any shortcomings. To gain their insight on how you might better support them and guide them toward success, ask your team members for input.

For what reasons should managers evaluate their leadership style?

In order to establish methods to successfully support their teams and identify areas for improvement, managers benefit from conducting leadership style assessments.

2. Establish a shared vision To create a shared vision for the future, work with your team. Identify goals and objectives together, and then coordinate everyone's efforts to achieve them.

What is the benefits of establishing a shared vision with your team?

Creating a shared vision strengthens the team's sense of ownership and accountability while assisting in coordinating everyone's efforts toward accomplishing shared goals and objectives.

3. Set clear expectations: Ascertain that team members are aware of their roles and duties and what is expected of them. To keep them on track, clearly state goals and

objectives and offer regular feedback.

How can clear expectations help to support team success?

Team members can better understand their tasks and roles when there are clear expectations for them. This can enhance the performance of the entire team as well as productivity and efficiency.

4. Encourage open communication: Promote open communication among team members and show a willingness to consider criticism and recommendations. Encourage a respectful, trusting environment where team members can freely express their opinions.

Why is open communication important for team success?

Open communication promotes the exchange of ideas and comments within the team and helps to establish trust and respect. Better decision-making, more inventiveness, and higher levels of team spirit can result from this.

5. Foster collaboration: Provide opportunities for team members to collaborate and exchange ideas to promote cooperation and collaboration. Encourage cross-functional cooperation through breaking down silos and rewarding teamwork.

How can collaboration support team success?

Silos can be broken down through collaboration, which also promotes cross-functional teamwork, which can raise output, enhance problem-solving, and improve decision-making.

6. Empower team members: Provide team members the freedom and tools they require to take charge of their job and make decisions. While giving them the freedom to take risks and learn from their failures, you should also coach and support them as necessary.

Why is it important to empower team members?

Team members that are empowered have the freedom and tools to take responsibility for their job and make decisions. This might result in more inspiration, imagination, and innovation.

7. Foster a culture of continuous improvement: Promote

a culture of continuous improvement by constantly

asking for input, reviewing the findings, and making

any necessary adjustments. Enjoy accomplishments,

but also be open to learning from mistakes and utilizing

them as growth-oriented opportunities.

How can a culture of continuous improvement support

team success?

A continuous improvement culture pushes the team to

review findings frequently, get feedback, and adjust as

necessary. As a result, efficiency, output, and team

performance may all rise.

ABOUT THE AUTHOR

As an innovative and dedicated trainer and instructor in the field of Business and IT with over 25 years of experience, I am committed to helping, supporting, educating, and inspiring students and co-workers to succeed. Throughout my career, I have successfully planned and implemented all phases of training development programs and held various positions such as Instructor, College Dean, and Officer in Training

Development. In my 7 years of experience as a Staff Affairs &
Training Development Officer, I demonstrated my ability to
manage and develop training programs that cater to the needs
of diverse individuals. I have also spent 8 years managing a
team of IT professionals, ensuring quality service delivery
across the University of Technology and Applied Sciences. I
bring a wealth of knowledge and skills from my 10 years of
experience as a Business and IT Instructor. I possess excellent
communication skills, interpersonal abilities, organizational
skills, and leadership skills. I am also adept in project appraisal
and evaluation and have a keen attention to detail, decision-
making abilities, and critical thinking skills.

References

Lu, J., Wang, X., & Wu, X. (2020). Team mindset and team

innovation: The mediating role of psychological safety. Chinese

Management Studies, 14(3), 527-541.

https://doi.org/10.1108/CMS-06-2019-0248

Spreitzer, G. M. (1995). Psychological empowerment in the

workplace: Dimensions, measurement, and validation.

Academy of Management Journal, 38(5), 1442-1465.

https://doi.org/10.5465/256865

Morrison, E. W., & Milliken, F. J. (2000). Organizational silence:
A barrier to change and development in a pluralistic world.
Academy of Management Review, 25(4), 706-725.
https://doi.org/10.5465/amr.2000.3363311

Edmondson, A. C. (2012). Teaming: How organizations learn,
innovate, and compete in the knowledge economy. John Wiley
& Sons.

Kearney, E., Gebert, D., & Voelpel, S. C. (2009). When and
how diversity benefits teams: The importance of team
members' need for cognition. Academy of Management
Journal, 52(3), 581-598.

Tjosvold, D., Tang, M. M., & West, M. A. (2004). Reflexivity
for team innovation in China: The contribution of goal
interdependence. Group & Organization Management, 29(5),
540-559.

"Sayyid Asaad bin Tariq meets South Korean foreign minister"
(Oman Observer, October 7, 2021):

https://www.omanobserver.om/sayyid-asaad-bin-tariq-meets-
south-korean-foreign-minister/

"Oman's Special Representative for Foreign Affairs and Asad

Bint Tariq Al Said meets Afghanistan President" (Times of

Oman, August 31, 2021):

https://timesofoman.com/article/104928-omans-special-
representative-for-foreign-affairs-and-asad-bint-tariq-al-said-
meets-afghanistan-president

"Duqm project attracts over OMR 12bn investment" (Oman

Observer, March 8, 2021):

https://www.omanobserver.om/duqm-project-attracts-over-
omr-12bn-investment/

"Oman's Special Representative for Foreign Affairs meets

Iran's FM" (Times of Oman, January 11, 2021):

https://timesofoman.com/article/oman-special-
representative-for-foreign-affairs-meets-irans-fm

Corporate Culture Pros. (2022). Google Corporate Culture.

https://corporateculturepros.com/google-corporate-culture/

Johnson, L. (2021). How Amazon Creates A Culture Of
Innovation. Forbes.

https://www.forbes.com/sites/forbestechcouncil/2021/05/1
9/how-amazon-creates-a-culture-of-
innovation/?sh=3d3eb82278f1

IBM Institute for Business Value. (2017). Collaboration at
IBM: An Interview with Luis Suarez. MIT Sloan Management
Review. https://sloanreview.mit.edu/article/collaboration-at-
ibm-an-interview-with-luis-suarez/

Medium. (2019). Innovation at Apple: Lessons from Apple's
Most Innovative Companies.

https://medium.com/swlh/innovation-at-apple-lessons-from-
apples-most-innovative-companies-2a8d4edcfb72

Harvard Business Review. (2019). Inside Microsoft's Culture of
Continuous Learning and Improvement.

https://hbr.org/2019/05/inside-microsofts-culture-of-
continuous-learning-and-improvement

Omantel. (2017). Taqdeer: Your Idea, Our Innovation.

Retrieved from

https://www.omantel.om/About%20Us/Taqdeer

Oman Air. (2019). Wijdan. Retrieved from

https://www.omanair.com/en/about-us/wijdan

Bank Muscat. (2019). Mabrouk. Retrieved from

https://www.bankmuscat.com/en-
us/AboutUs/Pages/Mabrouk.aspx

Petroleum Development Oman. (2018). Tanfeedh. Retrieved

from

https://www.pdo.co.om/en/Corporate%20Social%20Respons
ibility/Tanfeedh/Pages/default.aspx

Oman Refineries and Petrochemicals Company. (2019). i-

Enhance. Retrieved from https://www.orpic.om/en/About-

Us/i-Enhance

Walmart. (n.d.). Sustainability. Retrieved from

https://corporate.walmart.com/sustainability

Walmart. (2016). Walmart's sustainability journey. Retrieved

from

https://corporate.walmart.com/newsroom/2016/11/17/wal

marts-sustainability-journey

Sroufe, R. (2013). Walmart's sustainability strategy (C):

Inventory management in the seafood supply chain. Journal of

Business Strategy, 34(5), 41-50. doi: 10.1108/JBS-03-2013-

0023

Oman Oil Refineries and Petroleum Industries Company

(ORPIC). (n.d.). Sustainability. Retrieved from

https://www.orpic.om/en/sustainability

Oman Observer. (2018). ORPIC receives sustainability award.

Retrieved from https://www.omanobserver.om/orpic-

receives-sustainability-award/

Muscat Daily. (2018). ORPIC wins sustainability award.

Retrieved from

https://muscatdaily.com/Archive/Oman/ORPIC-wins-

sustainability-award-5b75

www.ingramcontent.com/pod-product-compliance
Lightning Source LLC
Chambersburg PA
CBHW072150230526
45467CB00042B/1605

* 9 7 9 8 3 8 7 6 3 0 7 5 0 *